How To Wipe Your Butt For Kids

A Simple, Step By Step Toilet Training

Written by: Tasha Powers and Steven R. Graham
Illustrator: Tran Dang

To Eric, Milah, and Landon and to the Occupational Therapy Community who gave me the opportunity to work with children everyday.

Let's Play and Learn!

Visit www.tashaspttoolbox.com to get exclusive access to super fun play activities that promote toileting hygiene independence:

- Peanut Butter Balloons Activity
- Hand Strength & Coordination Activities
- Trunk Range of Motion Activities
- A list of Adaptive Equipment for wiping
- And Much More...

I went to grandma's house and she made me a **PB&J**.

As I finished eating, I said "Oh grandma, by the way...

I can finally use the toilet all on my own,
so does that mean you'll take me to get an ice cream cone?"

Grandma asked "How do you do it?" and I replied,
"There's not much to it...

It's pretty simple you see,
this is exactly what I do when I go poop and pee...

I just went poop and there's nothing left,
no stragglers, no drips.

I know my butt is dirty,
as I let out my final rips.

If I don't wipe my butt clean,
I can spread germs and that would be mean.

Other kids won't want to play with me,
if I'm stinky and smell like poop and pee.

As I stay seated on the toilet seat,
I reach to grab 4 pieces of toilet paper and fold them nice and neat.

As the smell lingers,
I place the folded toilet paper flat on my fingers.

I lean forward reaching behind my back,
on the same side as the hand I'm using to wipe deep within my crack.

And always remember to wipe front to back.

I wipe front to back applying deep pressure,
because I know if I do this right, I will only smell fresher.

As I check the toilet paper and see poop,
I fold it once more and make another swoop.

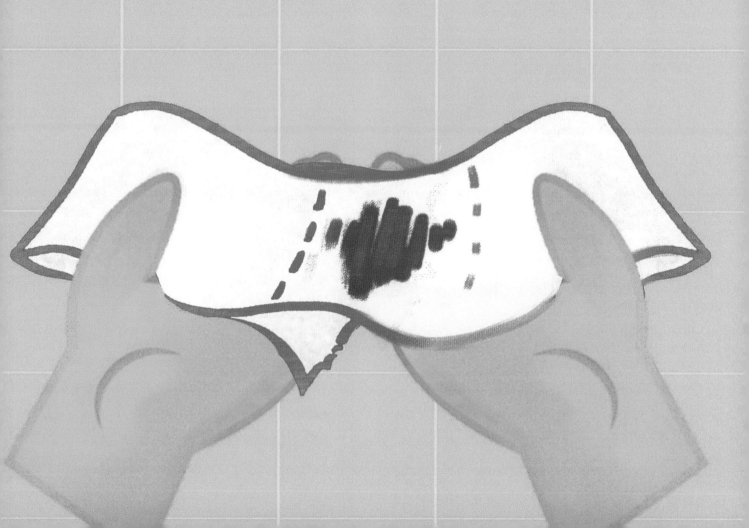

I always make sure I don't get poop on my hands,
or else I know it'll ruin my plans.

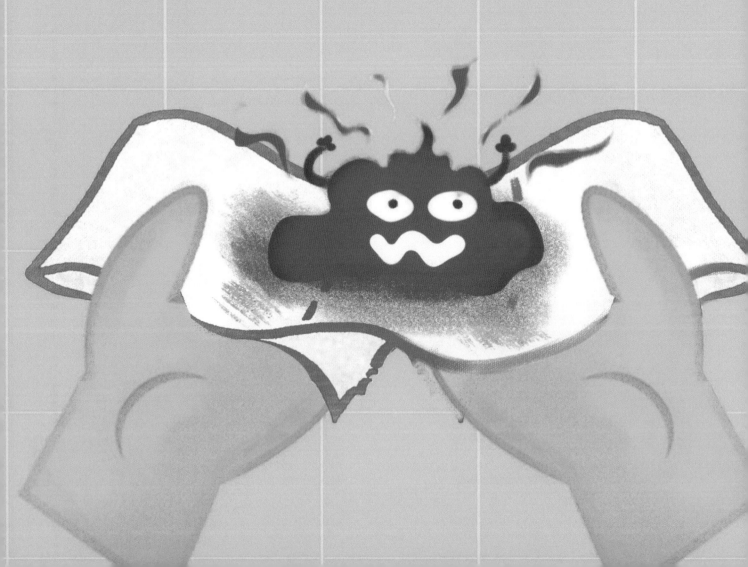

As I wipe my anus,
I gently press the toilet paper into the dark hole that looks like it leads to Uranus.

I take another look at the toilet paper
and see that it's mucky,
so I fold it a second time and wipe again
because I don't like feeling yucky.

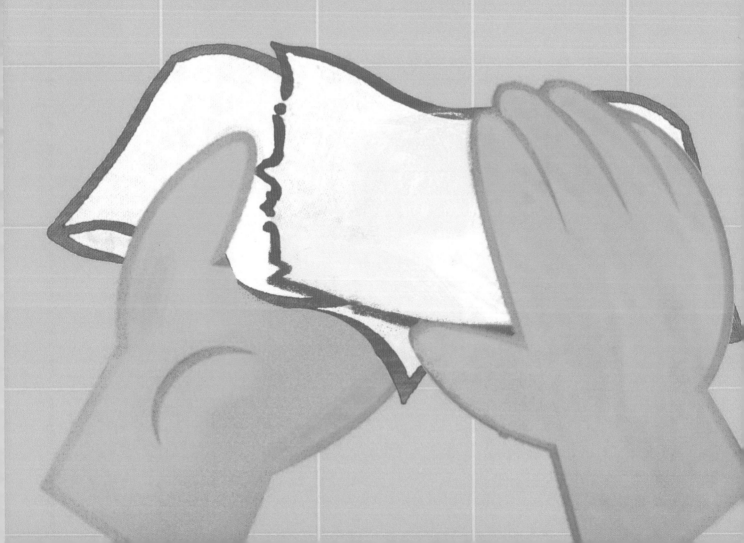

I check the toilet paper and still see just a little bit of poop, so I know it's time to give it one last scoop.

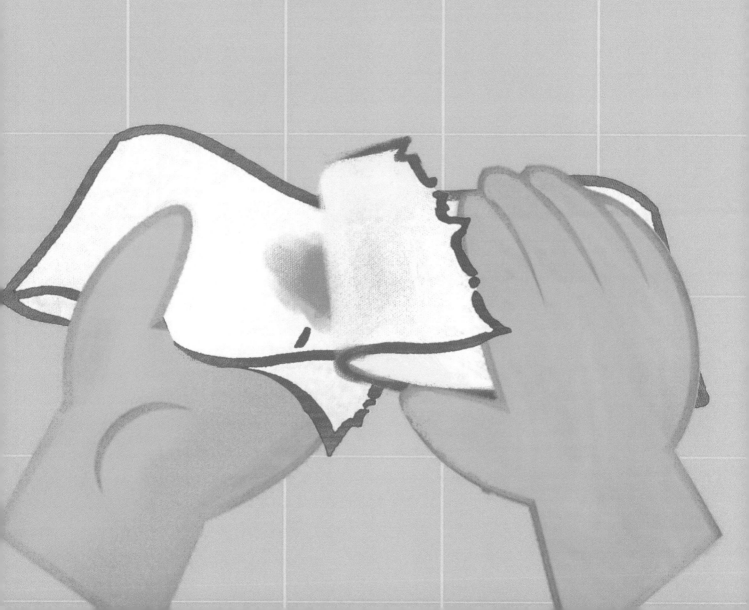

But this time I ran out of clean spots on the toilet paper,
so I drop it in the toilet and let it disappear like vapor.

I grab 3 pieces of toilet paper this time,
as I prepare to wipe away the remaining grime.

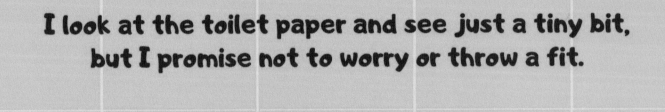

I look at the toilet paper and see just a tiny bit,
but I promise not to worry or throw a fit.

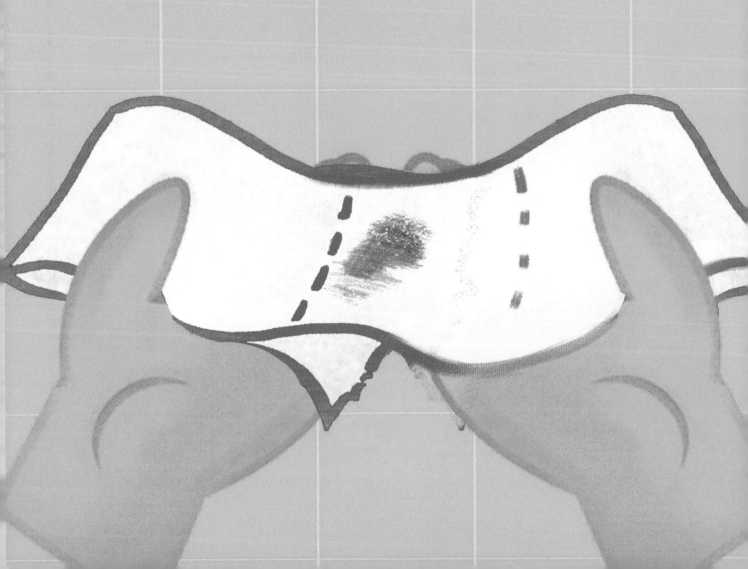

I must keep wiping until the toilet paper is clean,
or else this will start to become obscene.

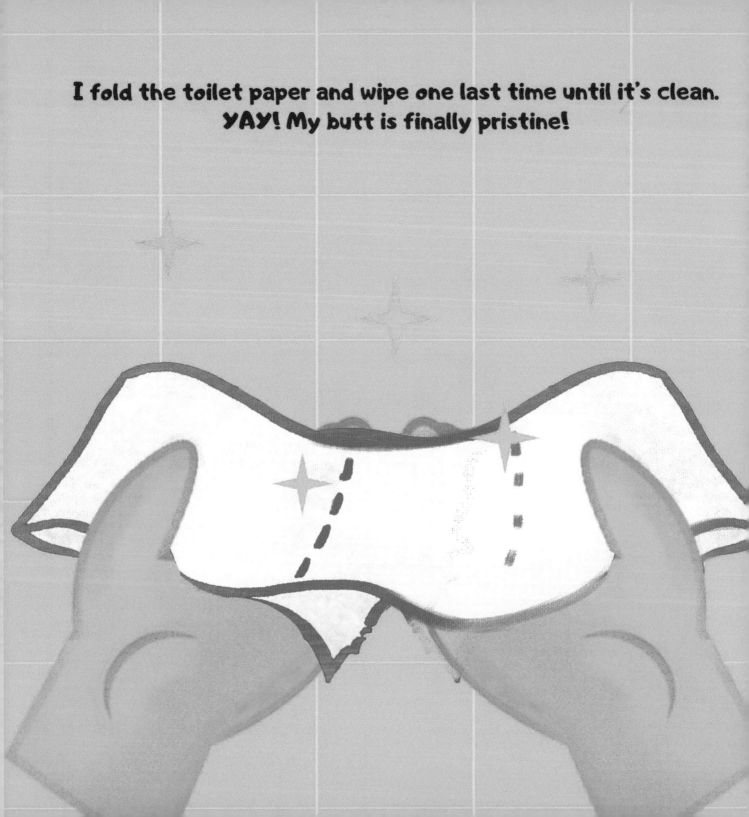

Once I'm done, I stand up,
pull my pants up, and make sure to fasten up!

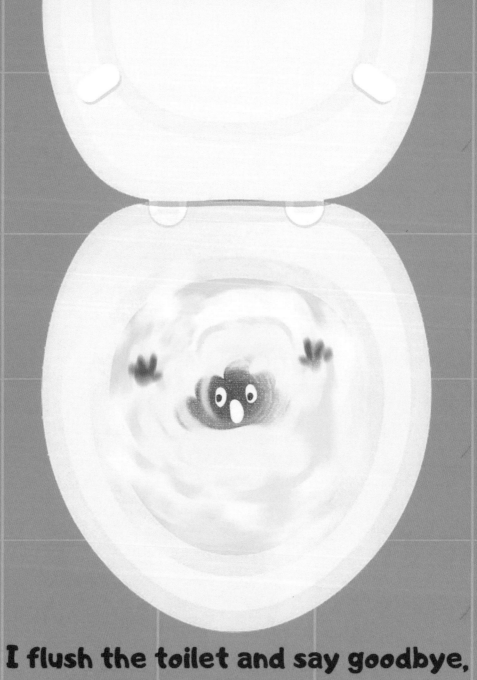

I flush the toilet and say goodbye,
to all the little poop guys.

I wash my hands with soap and water,
now that I know I'm a master squatter.

I make sure to scrub between my fingers and under my nails because I know this process never fails.

I scrub for at least 20 seconds and sing,
making sure my hands are super clean,
as I've finally become a pro at this routine.

Then I dry my hands with a clean towel,
and the peace of mind knowing they no longer smell foul.

I leave the bathroom feeling confident and clean,
as my parents cheer me on, making a scene."

Grandma looks over at me with a smile on her face,
now knowing that I can use the toilet on my own with such grace.

She then smiles and says,
"Now that I know you can stay clean,
I will take you to go get some ice cream."

If you learned a thing or two,
on how to wipe after a doo-doo,
would you be so kind and leave a review ?

Thank you

About Tasha Powers & Steven R. Graham

Tasha and Steven are creators of life-changing toilet training books for parents, "The Holy Grail of Potty Training" and children "Now I Know, How to Go Potty."

Tasha has worked with hundreds of children as a pediatric Occupational Therapist Assistant to achieve their individualized toileting goals on a daily basis.

Steven R. Graham is a visionary who is very passionate about teaching children to grow with a stable, strong, and positive mindset. His mission is to promote positive self-esteem and a healthy perspective on life through his books.

They are both passionate about promoting independence and enriching the lives of the little people who are going to go on to shape the future of our society and our world.

A message from Tasha:

Hey there! Come visit our website www.thiskidsfuture.com to get free toilet training books and exclusive toilet training resources that will help you get your little one trained quickly!

See ya there! :)

Cheers to toileting independence,
Your Expert Toilet Trainer Tasha

Printed in Great Britain
by Amazon